salmonpoetry

Publishing Irish & International
Poetry Since 1981

Revenant

CLARE McCOTTER

Published in 2019 by
Salmon Poetry
Cliffs of Moher, County Clare, Ireland
Website: www.salmonpoetry.com
Email: info@salmonpoetry.com

ISBN 978-1-912561-65-0

Cover Artwork: *Christophe Bonnière – 'Canada Goose, The moment of being airborne'*
INTERIOR IMAGES:
SECTION I – *Christophe Bonnière: 'Canada Geese, Break of dawn joy flight'*
SECTION II – *Susan Merrell: 'McAllister Street Pigeon'* © *Susan Merrell, 1998*
SECTION III – *Stieglitz, Alfred (1864-1946): Georgia O'Keeffe-Hands and Horse Skull, 1931. Gelatin silver print, 19.2 x 24 cm (7 9/16 x 9 7/16 in.). Gift of Georgia O'Keeffe, through the generosity of The Georgia O'Keeffe Foundation and Jennifer and Joseph Duke, 1997 (1997.61.37). New York, Metropolitan Museum of Art. © 2019. Image copyright The Metropolitan Museum of Art/Art Resource/Scala, Florence, Italy.*
Cover Design & Typesetting: *Siobhán Hutson*

Printed in Ireland by Sprint Print

*Salmon Poetry gratefully acknowledges the support of
The Arts Council / An Chomhairle Ealaíon*

In memory of Anna McAllister

(Goose)

1997-2014

Acknowledgements

All the poems in this collection have been previously published. The author would like to thank the editors of the following journals: *Abridged, Algebra of Owls, Boyne Berries, The Cannon's Mouth, Crannóg, Cyphers, Envoi, The Galway Review, The Honest Ulsterman, Iota, Irish Feminist Review, The Linnet's Wings, A New Ulster, Panning for Poems, Poethead, Poetry24, Reflexion, Revival, The SHOp, The Stinging Fly,* and *The Stony Thursday Book.*

The Ghost of 'lectricity howls in the bones
of her face and these visions of Johanna
are now all that remain.

BOB DYLAN
'Visions of Johanna'

The bones seem to cut sharply to the centre
of something that is keenly alive
on the desert ...

GEORGIA O'KEEFFE
'About Myself'

Contents

I

II

III

Christophe Bonnière: *'Canada Geese, Break of dawn joy flight'*

I

Goose

in memory of Anna McAllister

Walking evenings stretched out
into a prairie of stars
it seemed crimson and gold
would not rise
through bark and bole
and the goose following celestial cues
in the music of the spheres
would never leave
the soft bed
you spun for her
compassed by a newly hatched sun.

Falling like the bitterest snow
the moult had been hard
leaving her weak
till tail feathers
started to bud
on a harvest moon's pink edge
its strange light
striking lodestones
behind dull eyes
sparked the fires of flight
ancient watchers
of southern skies had described.

Navigating night's ametrine heart
she left without a word
each wing flap creating uplift
for those trailing after
on a journey
to the land of musk ox white bear
arctic hare and fox
drawn along

earth's magnetic course
she separates milk from water
feeding on pearls
deep in the silvery reeds
back once more in her true north.

The Soul Maker

for Ann McGill (née Quinn)

Year the blue planet's icy moons
stole the show
and a Tibetan pony nosed
the starry heavens
she came at harvest equinox
carrying copper scales
brilliantly balanced
with corn and snow-swept feathers.

On a black mineral glittered island
she was taught
all the holy places' names
safest paths
the purest stream
running through meadows
where she planted
a silver ring among wild poppy seeds.

Patch of carmine becoming garden
tilled from the hour of the hare
to night's fringe
by hands that fed the dark goose
sedge roots
and mosses, helping it
leave the gently lake-lapped grasses
for its wide unfettered north.

Gentian and larkspur and columbine
spreading with scarlet vine
to other grounds
blur the boundaries
she crossed
travelling in the storm's bright eye
all the way out to the marshes
just to glimpse the otter's silky length.

The Hungry Ghost

I was wondering about Van Helsing
the Ferrous Fumarate just aren't cutting it.
She has returned
crawled out of the hills
her translucent skin
scorched in a white summer moon.

I have reminded her of her death
explained the causes
spoke of obsequies carried out to the letter
wrote in black ink
you have gone forth, all the time
her green gleaming eye glancing my throat.

I have seen her bones in hard frost
heard the ceaseless howl
of her swollen silvery stomach
on bad nights left offerings
of milk and marigolds
at the edge of a spinney of mountain pine.

I used to think her kind could be stilled
with incantation and flowers
palm oil and bowls of bright feathers
but the souterrains
of her jealousy and greed
require the warm lapping of an open vein.

Times I was able to spare a pint or two
even dupe with red berry mojitos
and bloody Marys
now with her guile grown
and my haemoglobin at an all time low
I need her gone for good from this rickety door.

Then perhaps I could grieve
listen to Mozart's Requiem, Patsy Cline
or *Time Out of Mind*
even dislodge this bolus
of large and little lies, the threats of self harm
spangling my craw like a scrannel of stars.

It is time for the Heimlich manoeuvre
Van the main man very man for the job.
Once my breathing is freed-up
he will encircle me
with Eucharist and words in Latin
and oil heated in fires rendering injured icons.

Glad when her footprints fade from these streets
I will leave no alms
at the town gates
no orris root no food no wine
and ask no diviner
if hard snows will come to the high stony ground.

Neruda's Exhumation

Margaret Thatcher's eyes
closing today in the Ritz Hotel
seemed to open his
in the dry salty air
of Chile's volcanic coast.
His shining bones
washed anew
in a ravenous blistering blue
rise up again
to the welcoming strains
of a dusty-suited string quartet.

Playing within earshot
of old ships' mermaids
suspended like ghosts mid-flight
round the house
he dry docked
on that rocky outcrop.
Home to collections
of seashells
strange shaped bottles
bowls of bright green words
used to staunch
the blood
flowing from a wound
in the desert's starry side.

Its long silvery scar
snaking through planets
and paper lanterns
flickering with his passage
from crashing Pacific.
To government lab
reading bones
before second burial.

Day of the first
crowds thronged the streets
sorrow streaming down
black and white photos
but how long
do people weep,
one thousand days or one?
Hiding gypsy prayers
in a cello's flaming mane
some weep still
weeping till emerald ink leaves
a pure white page.

The Exhumation of Elizabeth Siddal

It was five minutes before midnight
when the knock came to my Highgate door.

Howell, washed in white moonlight,
took a good gawp then snatched the poems.

Startling to be sure yet scarcely a surprise
I always knew he'd want them back.

Truth told, I wasn't sorry to see them go
the calf-skin cover had chaffed my ear

for the best part of seven years.
Between ourselves, I hadn't read a single line

the light in here being bleedin' woeful.
But don't get me wrong, he meant well enough.

I even half-hoped he might appear, lured by
the prospect of a face wan with waiting.

Supreme *Beata Beatrix* sequel painted plein-air
the apotheosis of a pre-Raphaelite woman:

languorous bones, long and lovely on teal silk,
in a coffin full of red-gold hair.

Disarticulation

in memory of EM

For them the grave gave no rest.
Solely a spot to have and hold
not visit on stormy nights
with avellana and white lupin.
Their beloved kept above
the inscrutable depths.
Each light-riddled skeleton
dispersed near and far
along slender paths
in groves of mountain thorn
among the forest's earth stars.
Scattered bone shrines
leaving the departed free to wander
across space and place and time.

Out there in the raven Mesolithic
would they have buried you
with ochre and antler
deer teeth, flint and amber?
Far from settlement
on an island low in brackish water
would they have fanned flames
to seal the grave's scarlet lips?

Back in our un-velveted sixties
dying the wrong death
your own was dug in liminal land.
Striking distance
of font and altar and magenta
gold and indigo glass
the tract where they lowered you
our dangerous dead.

But soon unearthed bones
will gleam in a blue Bedouin moon.
Humerus ulna radius
set on the valley's wind-scoured floor.
Femur fibula tibia
high on dry northern chalk.
Mandible and skull
without blessing stone or feather
here above bog and pine
and old ghost trains.
Alone where the watch bitch walks.

Sky Burial

They are burning juniper incense
to summon bald headed angels
holiest of birds
waiting impatiently
on high charnel ground.
As double-sided hand drums
and incantations chime.
Well above the orchid tree line
frayed messaline soil
covers hard packed crystal frost
and a bed of solid rock.
Some others transfigured
into air back into thin air
would have bought
if they could
pyres of cypress
larch and dragon spruce.
From early youth
her choice:
alms for sky dancing carrion —
pale-faced vulture, crow and hawk.
Small prey still among snow lotus
highland hare, vole and shrew
let live another day.
Now in high spirits
the body breakers,
their work done
with ritual flaying knife
and axe and sledge,
mix for the wakeful griffons
ground bone, sweet milk
and roasted barley.
While the yak that carried her,
released into the crack of dawn,

crosses a wide plateau
ghost winds riffling the hem
of his great black coat.
Cold as a stone slab
where livor mortis,
shadowing flesh with lapis lakes
and pools of gentian, proved
what she always knew
death is the colour of ascension.

Bone Constellations

in memory of Maggie O'Brien (née Flanagan)

In a graveyard searching among the stars
for the bones of a woman
dead over thirty years
I see something glimmer
on the floor of the water carrier's jar.
It could be a femur, tibia or fibula
long bones in a pitcher of sky.

If reaching could draw them down
to where time and patience
perfectly placing each turn all
to a cathedral of white opaline
I would ask the wisest in these woods
to thrum up flesh and blood
with a low-voiced journeying drum.

Calling you back to the far hill
you walked with a small bird man
the tart-tongued said
you should have been glad to get.
And there we might speak
of mornings at your well
ankle-deep in pale-blue larimar light.

Under a roof of rented tin
talk might turn to a mare's amber eye
to the final tear you cried
to nights you walked
a high path through whins and ice
leaving what offering with your God
half hawthorn tree half Christ.

Wren

Driving to Bellaghy today, wondering why?
It's not like I knew you
or would,
had chance crossed our paths,
said the words
standing now
beside your sycamores I cannot.

My stumbling block, seriously, your first name
so instead of talk
I study the plot
glar behind thorns,
crumbling headstones left nearby
their tiny narratives
gone with the weather. And pulpy
in tawny veins
a tree's blood carrying flesh up
to a luminous beyond.

But not a breath broken
until, 'Jheezus Seamus there's a wren'
and there it was
somewhere between
your low umbery laugh
and my shoulder
its tail a pencil stub, the beak
a sharpened nib
delving deep
an old marker's mossy crevice.
For you
forager of the broken
no better ground.
Troglodytes troglodytes
leaving the lark to dig the depths of blue.
Maestro of the dark.

Saint Teresa's Heart

Claiming it a charism
too diamond for the dark
they hung her heart
out to dry in a glass globe.
Scored and scraped
with a life story
the walls of its chambers
reverberate still.
A girl calling out
to another
inscribes amber swallows
and nival lilies
on woodwork
no one can unravel.
A mystic
with inquisitorial
breath brimming
the nape of her neck
etches on stone
he has no body but my own
immaculate and shining
in fields of barley
this flesh has flown.
A nun crossing
night's cedar soul
writes on an acre of snow
O my sisters
this I left
leaving only entrails
filled with stars
and garnets.
An old woman
contemplating
a wide geranium sky

pencils in its margins
morning has come
all is light and all are
inexorably pierced
peregrine and moons
circling earth's fine tilth.

Saint Christina's Gut

Of all the trees my favourite
this sea-green turning silver pine
roosting me among the stars
the strength of its scent
sapping the stench
of their flesh and their gold.

Hunched on the top branch
I am a sparrowhawk
female of the species
larger by far than any male.
Today I have fed well
on the prey he could not take.

I, my own cartographer
up here with my book of maps
comping high contours
in charcoal chords.
Under this cape my dewy breasts
swollen with lapis lazuli.

Out at the end of a birch twig
I am an ortolan bunting
my song winding
its way past the sun
a thousand pinpricks of light
bursting from seeds in my craw.

No holy anorexic I gorge
on the tufted heads of thistles
in the lavender fields
in fields of millet
vittles needed navigating night
on my long journey south.

High among incensed rafters
I am a pigeon sunk on the hoops
of my nacreous skirts.
This scavenged gut
a neap tide warm and lapping
the edges of magenta feet.

Saint Joan's Mirror

Pouring over her
like amethysts and water
the voices
tell how she glowed
white and gold
walking with night's dead
in doublet and hose.

Whispering *we know*
breast buds bruise
plaits hiss, mirrors sicken
they slip away
in snowdrifting petals
leaving her luminous
in the garden of almonds.

She will put the Dauphin
on the throne
rise the *fleur-de-lys*
over Orleans
and in male attire still be
their astral child
inviolable in the last pond of sky.

Mary Magdalene's Foot

Pilgrims kiss
the window in this silver shoe
seeking blessing or cure
from flesh once witched
by the beauty
of a road travelled
with Mary of Bethany and Salomé.

A wanderer then
casting my sandals off before entering
the fields of the forest
the footprint
left beside morning's stone
a weathered intaglio
washed with wild hyssop and water.

Washing others
on the shores of the black harp sea
I was the starry diviner
and in eastern light
the myrrh bearer
my insouciant sapphire heart
freer than any in Samaria or Judea.

Some stormy season
this small window will shatter
returning me
to the holy ground
my fingertips reaching out
to the pines and hawks
my sole firm on the dark mineral earth.

Julian's Eyes

*All shall be well and all shall be well
and all manner of things shall be well*

JULIAN OF NORWICH

She did not drink dark cups from the sores of the dying
feed the destitute or found an order.

Bernini did not trace the arc of her spine
sculpt her sigh

or tease out the sweetness of her fiery entrails.
In a stormy seaport she saw, that is all.

The remaining years spent in an anchorite's cell
sounding the depth of her vision

till touching the loveliness of its nacreous floor
she wrote: do not accuse yourself of sin

behovely, it lanterns the stones of your wrath.
And of this be sure

wrath has no breath but your own.
The father no entity, only place

where winds stir the high green grain.
And a mare swims across the lake's sunstone face.

Our Lady of Częstochowa

Not one to meet on a dodgy side street
Częstochowa is a hard looking case
round the block more times
than she cares to recall
some claim her canvas a tabletop
painted by Luke the Evangelist.
Carried in a blanket
over wintered fields and lakes
to a village shrine.
Placed there to guide and guard
every man woman child
golden grains and heavy horses
their dancing flocks of white strokes.

Not ones for faffing around
the Hussites hit the ground running
shedding icon blood to sap self
laying low sanctum and soul.
With two deep scars
gullying face eye to jaw
slashing swordsmen
thought her well and truly done for.
Fooled by mossy breasts
and robes of iris *fleur-de-lys*
they could never have guessed
how well the bitch on the shelf
could handle herself.
Czarna Matka The Black Madonna
Queen of the Heavens
Mother of Earth, Star of the Sea
Hodegetria She Who Shows the Way.

Her right hand pointing at her son.
His straight back at her.

Guadalupe of the Cupboard

Altar piece in North Denver thirty-five years
without censure
then a new governor
slapped her in the cooler
for distracting hearts and minds
from the sacred sublime.
Our Lady of Guadalupe
quarantined with mops and brushes
has seen more solitary than Steve McQueen.

Finding in the soft syncresis of her mestiza face
something found no other place
the threshers of golden grains
lily growers
Azteca horse breakers
silver weavers, black clay shapers
called her Madre
since she jaded the Altiplano's winter skirt
with quetzal song and dahlias for Juan Diego.

Steady in azure upper arm tattoos
swinging from mirrors in battered Nissans
she's been with *Los Mojados*
every step of the way
from the border
jumped at Tijuana
to a forty-seven foot mural
banged up behind studs and laths
and milk-white plaster in a Coloradan chapel.

Talking straight the head honcho in the parish
told them it was all about the boy
the broad in blue had to walk
leaving the cross

a cameo square in snow
casting no shadow
on his own stone throne.
While Jesús sore and alone in night's red heart
stooping slips a note under her door.

Something Back

in memory of Julia McAteer (née McGuigan)

Today your daughter said everyone wants something back
the site she sold where an old house tilted like a womb
our now gone backfield that oblong of pristine green
the root of a lushing lilac bush earthed for a hundred years
a white-scarred gelding traded how many snows before

you died gaining in granite a syllable you never had in life
an absence filled with ibis and orioles and waxwings
your name in that girl's ear a rare fleeting foreign thing
you would never have claimed your own
you never did the two bedrooms sleeping five

the living room clean of ornament and antimacassar
the two postage stamps of grass separated by a short path
host to a boy hatching joy from a gnarled brush shaft
the books you read but did not own or want to own
circulating like wandering stars through silver poplars

their light barred always from your grandson's satchel
empty of paper and pencil those tools of an intellect
I doubt you would have wanted back
knowing his dawns break in water clear and deep and wide
no man with line and plumb will ever come.

Giving Voice To

Beneath the window blue morning glory and spit
spill from a girl's lips

on the floor
a boy shakes his head from side to side and groaning

glitters plants with the scent messages of wolves.
Over in the corner a young woman

gently slip sliding slip slip sliding
along the crest of an incontinence pad

throws back her head, sound
irised and molten pouring from her mouth.

In this place where the nonverbal dwell
speech is many:

spiral shrapnel ovoid rose.
Mine an Arabian cat hardest to catch of any

all claws and velvet it melts
into gold peninsular light.

Its small howl reminding mother father helper you are
not my voice.

The Ghost Orchid

Eldest of four children and the youngest too
he always seemed to fit.
His face in her hands a ghost orchid
her arms and lap
growing him the perfect bark
nothing touched
quite like his aerial roots, bright tinkling breath
his language of the forest and the stars.

Wondering at every leaving if he would wake
wanting her to come to him
with a cup of water
the guilt was there
scrabbing her skull when she went to work
or saw the moon luminous and full.
Its creamy claws stropped
giving consent finally for them to peg feed her boy.

No more smooth vanilla spinning gold on lips
never parting with a word or forming O
facing the benediction of virgin snow
no more broken bread, piloted
through jiggery egg and onion air.
Changed completely – secret Sunday afternoons
lemony with sherbet dip
crackly with salty potato crisps.
Each one a crescent of sparkling light on his tongue.

And when she thought he could lose nothing more
they said too weak for walks
from now on strictly wheelchair and hoist.
The ground she stood shifting
under that first lift, up there
higher than ever before

joy a chorus of cloud pouring from his mouth
thin white legs leap-frogging air.
The shots she always said he called, right on target:

Small shoulder blades pierced and glistening.
The afterbirth of a wing.

Comfort is Remembering

the perfume of petrol
dripping sickly sweet from his breath

the glue bag
suckled like a pungent sticky breast

the sludged speech
a shovelful of dingy sodden sound

the craquelure in faeces
hardened inside stonewashed Levis

the cornflower blue
turned ranting raving white rolling eye

comfort is not remembering
a buff jotter curled at the corners

the thick pencil
standing straight in a small podgy fist

the dragged nib
trying to hold letters between the lines

the foot of an L
wide enough to walk fostering fields

the i's head
dreaming sky in the depths of snow

the arm of an a
curving a consummate nothing

and from an m's lead steeps
the black wind howling down her veins.

Amy's Song

She is a raven
scavenging
burning stones and stars
standing somehow
in gallows drop stilettos
she touches again
dark red roses
scattered in a hurricane
of feathers
backcombed and wild
as moss-green eyes
spilling soul
and a soul's bones
in a version of black
I go back to
time after time
catching with my long lens
the darkness
pouring from her mouth
like a sash
of night in Camden Town
twisting turning
rising in crosswinds
till it falls
with the gone of it all
different from any
before or since. She was.

The Meaning of the Tiger

after India's Daughter

There is no way to start
to write to think of you leaving the cinema
possibly pondering the meaning of the tiger
crossing an ocean with a boy on a raft
a metaphor for the dark side of the self
or just a tiger red in tooth and claw.

Child you are waiting
beneath a Munirka moon swallowed in smog
you are waiting to board that bus
one swish closes the doors, soon
the magnolia tree will turn the colour of pain
your womb full of stars
falling one by one to their death.

Child is the only word
on a tongue that knows you are woman
fighting with broken nails and broken teeth
and broken screams, eviscerating fingers
trying to hollow you to fill nothing
the gnawing nothingness in themselves.

Silently glinting in night forests
the tiger is a solitary hunter,
rank with each other's stale seed and sweat
they hunt down quarry in a pack
their grunts and squawks unable to smother
the garnet glimmering in your throat.

Others would have morphined out
the consciousness you clung to those last days
possibly pondering the meaning of man
daughter of a mother
stooping in blue snowmelt
to trace on a high crescent Himalayan lake
the contours of your face.

The Light in Argenteuil

Has gone from Room 10 Merrion Square.
The black sun left by a puncturing fist
enshadows lozenges of lapis
light blue and aqua –
rapid broken brushwork
once shimmering
water and autumn's russet ghosts.
Drifting toward a village flecked with gold.

Transmuted now to a square of shade
on red embossed wallpaper.
His monument to the moment
spirited away
by a flock of hands
straining under swan neck lamps
to suture not restore.
Discharged light rendering canvas
dimmer than before that dawn that he caught
the transient luminous riverside.

His wild moth eyes full of violet
tracking protean prey
through field and orchard
and the garden
where he knelt in old age
planting iris
and rhizomes of light.
Shoots spread near and far
one stolen this year from a boat's white sail.

The perpetrator remanded in custody
same court same judge same day
a rapist is granted the bail he jumped
to flee the country
for the Continent.
A girl left wondering
what price placed
on the jagged shadow
that falls between her legs and will not still.

ECT

Back then they thought your head was cut.
Hurtling across the globe
one end's errand
to see a bird barely bigger than a fly.
And yes, you did
crouched starry-eyed in leaf litter
you saw it.
Day breaking over the hills
behind Cárdenas when it first appeared.
Zunzuncito, the bee hummingbird
shimmery and suspended in a bivalve of air.

Later on they knew your head was cut.
How could they not
it was written all over your arms
and breasts and thighs
body turned travelogue
its hieroglyphics deepening
with each chapter.
You got the works: Citalopram
Fluoxetine, Amitriptyline, Mirtazapine.
ECT finally doing the trick.

Electrical storms cooled now to fog
softening the edges
of sodium light, impulses and knives
but not the smell
of sweat on a greasy vest
not the taste
of roll ups on an old man's breath.
Some things are sharper
in this fog you know will never lift
some, like the bright-blue wing of a tiny bird
gone for good.

The Red Olinguito

You turned up in a drawer
in the Smithsonian
luxuriant in deep coral fur.
Samples and swabs
pokes and prods proving
beyond all doubt
a new species
could blaze a trail
lengthening lists
in museum catalogues
in mammalian taxonomies.

No time till they spotted
copper eyeshine
burning in the forests
you travel by night
drinking from flowers'
noctilucent mouths.
Solitary in misty canopies
shy fig-eating carnivore
smaller by far
than others
thought your kind.
Misidentified for years
now named
Bassaricyon neblina
round the hearth olinguito.

Thirty five years since
a mammal discovery
then two in two weeks.
First an omnivore
red in tooth and claw
yet so easily caught.

Standing for all to see
solo in spotlight
at Snaresbrook Crown Court.
Female of a species
renowned for
consummate cunning
and great guile
categorised sexual predator
formerly a child.

The Black Lark

after *I Know Why The Caged Bird Sings* by Maya Angelou

The breaking and entering
of an eight year old in yellow afternoon sun
sudden as love or hate.
Scimitar sundering through the eye of a needle
blinded by nothing it could name.
The terrible redundancy in his face
still shackling your tongue
long after slick-suited uncles
left him for dead.
Later seeing sullenness in silence
they lashed you too
sending you back to a grandmother in Stamps.
You liked her store best at dawn
waiting in slatted light to be opened
like a tabernacle or a heart.
Mute mornings
strung with pearls of promise
till doors unwrapped
the red dirt yard
you raked at night
drawing moons and stars and solar winds
in Arkansas soil.
Cinnamon constellations
circling a chinaberry tree
pledging shade
to barbers with glinting scissors
and scraping cutthroats
troubadours plucking juice harps
and twanging cigar-box guitars
cotton pickers come to buy canned sardines
sody crackers and peanut paddies.
You soundlessly serving
haloed in gold from a coal-oil lamp.

Your silence a shell
shielding that small sense of self
brittle body armour
nacreous the day she came
with a name
spilling apple blossom and Queen Anne lace.
Teacher telling you
flat words flush with page were half dead.
Reading poets old and new aloud only for you
chamois voice coloured azure and amethyst
each letter enweaved
syllables shelled, words unfurled.
What could you say when she asked you to speak?
Black lark rising from mother-of-pearl.

II

Susan Merrell: *'McAllister Street Pigeon'* © *Susan Merrell, 1998*

The Junior Room

in memory of Annie McGill

Annie's classroom was the only one in that small school
without pupils planted in rows
slicing the crumbly air straight as Christ's crucified stare.

Junior room sans roof sans floor was a lake of islands
slowly flowing from some geography of grace
in pale blues and milky opalescent silks.

Lanterned by liquid moon and serous stars floating
under the firmament of fish she fed with strange fruit
gathered down deep on the gravel's unmade bed.

Sediment stirred by flitting bats and the molten patterning
of their crystal chatter spreading as she held
between her thumb and fingertip a seed of water.

Swollen with three syllables sounded out
on a girl's new exercise book – pig-e-on. Turning to two
rising from the prow of an outrigger canoe.

The Tulip Weaver

for Anne O'Hagan

It is not the stars you got for them
beside A grades opening doors
to college campuses ochred with autumn
to libraries stacked with words
worked in agate and teak and graphite
to an almond thought
white inside night's solitary zenith.

It is not the landscapes you gave them
luminous in the east
where the first people of the book
study *halakha* and poetry
producing many sparks
where a gardener rolls back the stone
telling Magdalene speak to others
of what you have seen
where messengers with wings
circle the five pillars
zakat and *sadaqah* under Medina minarets.

It is not the lost gods you found for them
in stone and river and bark
their lidless eyes watching always
for return of some old believer.
What they remember most is the tulips
you wove for Judas
tumbling from your arms
threads of indigo and magenta and silver.

Mary of Fallagloon

in memory of Mary McKenna (neé McCotter)

The wedding name he gave
unused in our lowlands
where you are place.
Blanketing bog
gaunt supplicant thorns
beseeched amaranthine hills.
Sheltering three zinc-roofed
rain-serenaded rooms.

The rumour of furniture
two beds one wardrobe
and looming large
a rangy table
holding lessons
prepared at an oil lamp.
Grammar and composition
Greek and Latin roots
arithmetic, algebra, geometry
music and drawing.

Next to no interest
in those hasty concoctions
conjured in gurgling pots
stalwart on open fire
long after others
switched to stove switched
to shining enamelled cooker.

Your well-weathered door
always on the latch
no caller leaving
empty handed
cupboard scoured
for a brown egg
yellow pear or last blue fiver.

Sharp-suited cattle dealer brothers
only half amused
by the tall ship
sailing down Glenshane:
black hat clamped on
verdigris round rim
black overcoat
fastened with old safety pins.
Till heavy hems stilled
that night winds and stars
died out there among the marigolds.

Chairwoman

Slowly unwrapping her little layers every morning
we soap rinse dry from head to toe
deodorize her musk, perfume her neck and wrist
dress her in clean underwear
colour coordinating outer.
We dampen her hair
styling it the way we think best
we make her bed
chiseling out corners
lining up shells on the counterpane.
We call her dear, speaking her name over and over again.

Quickly crossing the dayroom floor we all hold hands
reminding her of the day month year.
Near the big blue chair
she birls round n n n   n n n n
n n n n n
drawing her knees up to her chest
she swings from our arms
like the ball on a strange executive toy h h h   hh   hh
words smithereened.

Safely strapped in, the air around her writhes
till hands wither
and hang exhausted from the recliner's arms.
Later we will rouse her for walks –
table – toilet – chair
capsizing her anew with each return.
But at the day's end
she is quiet.
In the lull between shifts, all is quiet.
The only sound a pen scratching:
Specialised seating as prescribed by medical officer.
Patient appears content. All care given.
Two brown eyes looking out of the dusk, bright and glazed.

Epsom, 1913

There is no way to escape this sarcophagus of hands
gripping my thighs, ankles, elbows
wrists, shoulders.
I am nailed to this rank bed
and already his fingers are inside
probing the gap
where he will thrust a metal screw
cranking my mouth wide open.
Waiting minute by minute
for that tube
to fill my mouth my throat
I cannot breathe
I am not breathing
I am drowning and will drown forty nine times more.

They do not know I was the girl with bright red hair
taking first class honours
in her Oxford finals
they do not care
I was the hard working teacher
paying her way fair and square.
Coming at the close of day
through grey clanking doors they will drown me again.

No stone in the midst of all, when all else failed
flesh and blood and bone
standing on the bank of a river of horses
minute by minute waiting
for the king's dark colours
minute by minute
on the crashing edge
plashing in at Tattenham Corner.

Too long a sacrifice
enchanting heart to globe
violet and luminous
pine-green and brimming silver starfish discharged
on the breast of a three year old colt.

An action firm and unfaltering
a scattering fissiparous and sparkling.

Fast

in memory of Cassie McCotter (née Mullan)

Stooped in an oil lamp's glow
a doctor with shirt sleeves
rolled up to the elbow
manoeuvred forceps
cold as anchor ice
the night you breach birthed
Augustine youngest child.
The bucky roses
that steel kiss left
on each temple
pulsed as the lion paced the purple heavens.

August big and blue
drifted high the Sunday you stood
chin resting on forearms
crossed on the chapel wall.
Going no nearer
to the grave receiving
seven summers
wrapped up in a little shroud.
There was no funeral mass
no officiating priest
just a sprinkling of undertaker prayers.

Today your howl would be hushed
with Citalopram or Mirtazepine
Fluoxetine or Cipralex
cognitive therapy or ECT.
Those days they'd have broken your fast
with funnels and feeding tubes
coiled like adders
on white enamel.

Some still say
he should have acted more decisively
taking the mountain road
in dusty black suit
and bespoke broad brim hat.
Quietly helping you out
of the Model T Ford
at the redbrick asylum's door.
Instead you stayed at home
lying with your face to the wall
in the dying room
clearing the ground
sweeping clean
the only space your boy had ever been safe.

Philip eldest son and water carrier
keeping ebony vigils by your side
offered food
on plate and saucer and spoon
silently about the time
the wild geese left
for he felt his pleadings
caused only distress.
Evenings brought your husband
to sit and speak
of the day's dealings
asking if you had eaten
without threat of institution
or treatment
jolting you to your senses.
Maybe he could see and maybe there are
some wounds that cannot be healed
some sorrows better to be
let be.

Something About Your Mother

for Conor Philip Leopold

Card came today telling me you loved that horse that rocks.
What can I tell you little adelaster bud?
Perhaps something about your mother, my mother's first grandchild
born with gold flowers in her mouth
named after a song at the end of desire.
A serious child from the start
holding silence in cupped hands like a damselfly's turquoise heart.
Silent still in a Belfast attic, head bent over Augustans and Romantics.
Till a sunstone compass pointed south.
Toward Miraflores and birdsong she loved and left
taking a deadbeat night bus across the Altiplano to drink black rum
in the Fallen Angel, camped with clouds at a gate to the sun.
And when the tropical storm broke laughing at Devil's Throat.
Happiest perhaps guiding that good bay mare
over wide shining Patagonian marsh.
Then Ushuiai down Tierra del Fuego way
sheathbill, tern, albatross
starboard baleens feeding on krill.
Ice hard hitting at Deception, near Whaler's Bay and Neptune's Bellow
channel choked with big bergs
waves washing her across the quarterdeck.
Repose restored following an old traveller's trail
(discussed a lot round here)
from standing moai and birdmen petroglyphs
lining world's omphalos
to Wellington to watch the white swan die.
Clocking *couru, déboulé, arabesque, arrière*
she thought Tchaikovsky totally metal
her own tested at Waitomo gliding endless glow worm caves.
Overwintering in Oz, grace that prompted a Maori chief
to gift a necklace of abalone and bone
taking her three hundred ks out of her way
dropping the Dutch hitcher at Jabiru.

Singing *One More Cup of Coffee* driving to Katherine
and after the rains, heavy on the pedal to Darwin
hitting the sands in time to dance
with flame-throwers at Mendil's midnight market.
But asleep beside a firefly river her dark ships drift back to Easter,
    and Jesus
tuning a Spanish guitar as she bleeds in the Atacama Desert
under Saturn's ice-craved moons.

Dream Hotel

The travelling man came back last night
with Dead Sea salt still in his hair.
We sipped a map or two
and trains began to flow down lines
that no train knew in fifty years.
With bag and polished route
we watched in creaking silence
for some approaching light
then rolling thunder rippled the night sky.
In the arms of a storm all transport died.
Rails rusted, propellers snapped, girths broke
the bay mare reared in white-eyed revolt.
Our roads, a carnival of turns
and unread glyptic paths, tined once more
when the door swung open
on a house I'd left half a life before.
In slow spreading lapis light
I saw its rooms and passages multiplied
a reception desk now stood
where heavy boots once dried.
My sister's crochet hook a stained quill
her exhausted jeans silk French flares
draped over the arm of an Art Deco chair.
Our ancient aunt, the dark colossus
who drove home a hatpin like a spear
transfigured with silver cigarette case
and Black Narcissus.
Out in the quartz gardens of this hotel
fissured with the living and the dead
a cold-footed northern swan glides past
on murmuring desert sands
as some of the thousand lives a life may lead
steadily unconceal.

On a Railway Platform

Lit only with a thin cedilla moon
he measures time by shadows
falling across tracks
once carrying
the finest cow-hide
raised in high country
straight to waiting cyclamen hands.

Crouching on a rickety stool
rangy and ragged
he is an eagle
in a checked seventies suit jacket
tight on broad shoulders
that recall that great coat
he wore walking
through a Hungarian winter.

The heels of knee high boots
leaving bespoke intaglios in snow
still on distant hills
when black stilettos came
lightly dusted
with Budapest summer.
Dreaming a world
before gladiator sandals
plimsolls, pumps and puma
the shoeshine man under Cassiopeia.

The Lunatic Line

The first Maasai medicine man saw it crawling
through his bones and whispering entrails
straight to a lake at the end of time. Before fish-plates

and fish-bolts, before a million sleepers buried
their heavy heads in dry rustling savannah grasses
two Tsavo males heard it coming from Mombasa.

Prophesied serpent larger than any ever seen
its iron jaws disgorging buffalo, eland, wildebeest
and all the tall white cattle in strange foreign lands.

Where men without skin strut sovereign soil calling
this space this time Europe in the late Pleistocene.
Ancestor, atavist, ape, ivory, coffee and tea

hauled forward down lunatic lines. The railway
worker's destiny manifest in the rhadamanthine iris
of The Ghost and of The Darkness.

Night Train

after *Man's Search For Meaning* by Viktor Frankl

At about midnight they passed
through a Viennese station
some standing some squatting in shifts
over scanty sodden straw.

From the dark side of a cattle car
he sees only night juddering
over the street where he lived
as a man and as a boy.

Onward toward the blue Danube
their breathless bones wait
for that first bridge crossing
straight to the heart of Mauthausen.

Passing it by exhalations escape
out through a thin slatted hour
the relief an aria
in black Bavarian night.

Rousing angels from rapture
to watch words on wintered breath
Dachau only Dachau only Dachau
plough a furrow to the stars.

The Paper Wall

Strained under a waistcoat's black satin
his spine crouches over
the last of the day.
It is summer in New York
pausing for a second
he blots his brow
the thermometer's artery
still throbbing
even though the ceiling fan
will soon jigger to a stop.
Writing *Declined* he wonders
if his daughter is asleep
her tiny fists crocus corms
dreaming under snow
by the time he gets home.
He will walk softly
from her room
checking all windows and doors
before listening to the news
on the big brown Philco wireless.
Chairs and *so longs* grate
the rustling air
clock decanting workers
into trilling Friday evening streets.
He signs his name
stretches and writes the date
setting on Anne Frank's visa application
a damselfly in a crystal half sun
paperweight.

Empty Ghetto

The leaving began at dawn.
Children put to sleep
with luminal, tightly packed
in handheld cases
others spilling shining
lumps of blue-black coal
or scraps of wood
emptied over balcony railings.

My gifts for the leaving
bromine and valerian root
and to the old, hair dye
ground from indigo and henna
that could not fool
the cool selectors filing
faces like apparitions
from some far-flung future.

Alone now in The Pharmacy
Under The Eagle
I sit among coloured bottles
stoppered ceramics
pestles and mortars used
to soften fear and knead
the edges of pain, compounding
codeine with a little hope.

The wind has left the pines
only rose-grey dusk remains
seeping through skylights
cupboard doors
piano lids, floorboards
filling stairwell, basement
bedroom, attic, tenement
deep in my cold stone bowls.

All the horses are long gone
the solitary sound
echoing these midnight alleys
my footfall in first snow
falling on silent streets
on a dead Zgody Square.
Covering a blue star
and couple of old kitchen chairs.

No Direction Home

From Rashidieh Camp an air-raid siren
scores southern Lebanon's graffitied sky
as Fatima sits with her back
to her shack's breeze block wall and recalls

snow-white souls of mulberry moths
and the high silvery hum
of leaves on each and every olive tree
suckling young and old on finest green gold

grown in Galilee's dusty grey ground
with figs and pomegranates and grape vines
entwined on solid two storey gables
bought and paid for with Palestinian pounds

saved in the tin toffee box she prises open
to show a British Mandate certificate
of ownership for a house in Umm al-Faraj
and nineteen dunam of land

taken by soldiers with scars in their eyes
and arms full of ashes.
O daughter, how goodly their tents
now a new moon scythes a meadow of stars.

The Empty Village

Rolling down the dirt road to Ein Hod
canvas on the big rattly truck
flaffs like a torn cloud.
Talk is of manifestoes
anarchy and impermanence
spontaneity and play
the native primitive restored.
Bohemians
to a woman and man
smoking Gitanes
wearing navy work clothes
descending on a village empty as dawn.

Its seven hundred year old symmetry
of site and structure
a found object
waiting in white excavated rock.
Small serpentine streets
cool courtyards
sweet with carob and fig
wild marjoram and geranium
drinking fountains
mystical stone houses
too quaint to disappear
brought back from the brink
by poetics and aesthetics.
Dadaism and dance performed in a mosque
remodelled on Café Voltaire.

Only a stone's throw from house-cum-studio
Janco painted frescoes in
whitewashed after Purim.
Dancing damsels
dogs, laughing heads, *Conversio*
the writing on the wall
restored with surgical scalpels.

Unconcealed had they dug
a little deeper
the place Abu Faruq touched
in forty-eight
leaving for the last time his home.
Forty-three years later
out in the dusty diaspora
he died a camp refugee
refused right of return
to pastures
buried beneath a sea of cyan pine.
Navigated by a modest couple in a sardine can.

Ghost Children

Do not waste your time hanging spirit traps
bright cloths hold no charm

nor offerings of pomegranate
left at the well with a jug of swan feathers.

Those stern geisha faces
cannot be lured out with such trifles.

They will remain dappling rubble
till the bulldozers and daisy cutters return

then carrying jimjams and limbs
and kittens by the scruff

they will leave their bombed out buildings
near sands where shells screamed

and curling up instead among weed trees
roughly rock each other to sleep

telling stories old people told
of homes with arris vaults and domical squares

farms grazed by long eared goats
of stony orange and lime and lemon groves

fleshy scarlet water melons
of stars for planting of moons for harvesting.

Covering them over with armfuls of leaves
we slip away before dawn wades in

to rattle spindly rib cages.
Shaking cold from their bones they will rise

some trembling some teasing
the little cephalophore shuffling around

with a frozen horned moon frown.
Dragging themselves up with the city

Gaza's ghosts will traipse again
down to the glittering sequestered sea

and silently watching know:
memory of a blue flax field shall be their coast.

The Memory Garden

In the heart of her garden
there is a seahorse
cherished from girlhood
she has fed it
the best blooms
scarlet pelargoniums
kaleidoscopic sweet peas
crystal blue lobelias
but now her little star has grown
dark as the day.

Its flowers are dying
choked with a calligraphy
of silvery slime
they struggle to survive
some last an hour
some a moment or two.
Brilliant summer bedding
she thought
vigilance and care
could preserve
later prayer and incantation
their names repeated time after time
over and over again.

In the heart of her garden
two almond trees
still speckle earth
their papery petals
a susurrus of wind song
making her weep
as she stoops
to pluck weeds from soil and gravel
tiles and carpet.

Round the heart of her garden
there is a great grey wall
its cracks and fissures
filled long ago with bellflowers
oracle sedums, red valerian
and the hart's-tongue fern
that just seemed to appear.
She knows they will go
they are going
fading one by one
one by one disappearing
even the flower opened
first in rose-gold Palestinian dawn.

By the wall of her garden
she listens to a lifetime's work
breathe its last
buds and leaves leaving
for the last time
without hope of return.
Soon she will see no more flowers
but she will hear
remember, she will hear
the chirrupy chatter of pinks
the velvet of gentians
the prattle of clematis
high above her head.
She can hear and will hear
in an otiose moon the cry of the rose.

Prayer for a Happy Death

They speak of her weight
the weather and the worms in her brain.
A captive audience
trying to deflect their words
with closed crusty eyelids
she traces butterflies spiralling in her skull.

Times there were flocks
Spanish queens, emperors, hermits, weavers
silver-washed fritillary
and from the far purple fields
a rare pearl in parenthesis.
Today one small cloud flits her mind's blue.

Scattering if rains come
a few graylings on her parched tongue.
Tinctured with the colours
of dusk and stone
one she truly wants
shutting pale wings vanishes in a crevice of bone.

Contracted forefinger
turned perch, finally coaxes *Invisible* down
sweetest communion of any
spreading spicy and molten
through her mouth.
Till a voice says *where the hell did that come from?*

A synapse must have sparked
somewhere.
Shaky and chapped
her dusty lips
summon a cardinal's prayer:
Lord take me home and letting me go let me go alone.

Wishing Back

I would not wish you back
to a place punctuated
with toileting
clothing and feeding
your lips laced up
at a small pink spoon's
plastic approach.

I would not wish you back
to the clattering
down of conversations
held over your head
or the sudden jolt
of a hoist
swishing from chair to bed.

I would not wish you back
to the barely damp
swabs keeping
your mouth half moist
or thick
truculent air
snatched in fits and starts.

I should not wish you back
to a huddled moment
heads may have touched
leaning into
a dark-blue dusky hour
me and you
trying to catch a word or two.

Stieglitz, Alfred (1864–1946): *Georgia O'Keeffe–Hands and Horse Skull, 1931.*

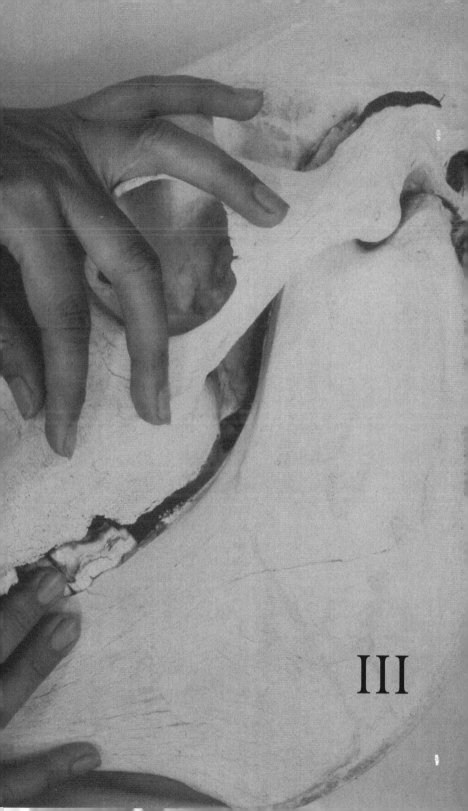

III

Shergar's Groom Wonders

What friends would think
if they knew
history is filtered
through the eye
of a horse
other times would have buried
in a bridle of brass
with grave goods at his muzzle.

Shergar's groom wonders
if those rebels
would have emptied a Mauser
into the river running down his face
or turned him loose
on mountain or meadow
slapping his rump
just for the hell of seeing him run.

Shergar's groom wonders
if his bright boy
expected car-lined afternoons
bookies shouting odds
a jockey punching air
being led up that rickety ramp
the night a soul-shaped thing
was glimpsed in frosted breath.

Shergar's groom wonders
if *Equus* could really be attuned
to the rhythms
of the human heart
his dark pulsings
the last
the horse heard
no other could have gotten so near.

Shergar's groom wonders
to this day where his bones lie
knowing they thought him
the perfect hostage
free from blood
they thought wrong
the horse
more brother than his father's son.

And he would have been made lovely
for the earth.

Whittling

From boyhood he had an eye for wood
reading sycamore and sitka spruce against the grain
he knew where to dip his hands into the shallows
scooping out rainbow trout and salmon.
It was all about patience, he said
kings of the Orient and stars and lambs and shepherds
coaxed to surface with small short strokes.
Knife more buff than blade
guiding stag out of oak that wanted to be deer.

Disappeared on August sixteenth nineteen eighty one
his was a long wake
push and pull motion paring flesh to bone
laid out in half-bog half-quarry three miles from home.
Twenty-nine years of Sunday searches
brought her a graveside
to shadow with time and worry-whittled skin.
Thin as each and every syllable they chip in granite –
it wasn't authorised by the leadership.

Gemini Grave

Will their bones remember
being a binary star
out in black
crisscrossed by tracks
of deer and vixen
and the honey-eyed hare.

Will their fingers remember
a sky of roots
quilting bone on bone
in a geometry
of curves and grooves
grown into down the years.

Will their spines remember
Meath's giving ground
and will they wait
for the call
of yellow bittern and raven
in their city graves.

The Messenger Pigeon

Black as a midnight archangel
by all accounts she was a rare bird
coming out of the east
with paltry papers
chancy class and creed.
None thought her a homer
those in the know
said she would never stay the pace.
Too lightweight for distance
too barnacled with birthings
to map the luminous lines
gleaming earth's magnetic fields.
Little did they think
she would come back
after three decades in sharp sand
on Shelling Hill Beach.
Minus massive orange bulldozers
or men in high viz jackets
she dragged herself up
navigating sound waves
and silvery scents
in a wild cartography of winds.
The iron particles
in her sun-infused compass
aligned north
bringing back to them
a crop of blue milk
and message carved on broken wings.
I am returned
I am returned I am returned.
And no more shall I part.

Disappearing Her Again

It happens in war
think Vietnam, Iraq

Afghanistan.
What happened her skin

her heart her hair
happens in conflict

       everywhere.

The Opal Miner

On the horizon of every dream
a play of colour
glimmers soil
heaving like a new birth.
This is a land
navigated by the stars
word of mouth and tattered maps.

In her eighth decade
feeling first frost
like never before
some say
she should leave the rough country.
Letting the opal lie
undisturbed in its thin crevice.

But how can she abandon
this dark place
needing more than ever
some kind of presence.
Not a god or feathers
just the bones of him
shoulder to shoulder in the earth.

Her dream was a long one
scraping back layer after layer
of Bragan Bog
till she found
a vein of adularescence.
Pale as her dove become bone
only the bones of a dog.

In the end the years carried her away
keeping covered up
what may shudder hearts
far off in time.
Having a method
or way with them to feel
the fear of the youngest disappeared.

Splinters

Out there where the crossing caravan
is a dark comet
they have discovered planets
beyond the solar system
measured the age of the oldest star
and spread a thousand red carnations
across the desert's frozen floor.

Three times this week she dreamed
a swallow nesting
in the eaves of his brain
leaves its clutch of speckled eggs
wakening each dawn
to the curled up memory
of a fairly ordinary Sunday afternoon.

The last one they spent at home
before he became a piece
in a black jigsaw
buried in the Valley of The Moon.
Its luciferous heart
pierced still with the shovel she gripped
day on dry day for seventeen years.

It could have been southern winds
forcing the Atacama's secret garden
to flower beneath their feet.
Splinters of rib and jaw
a scrap of cloth of shrivelled skin
and unfound
the nowhere relics of the disappeared.

Gathered together they are taken again
so science can make its mark
giving her back more than most
the shard of skull bone
she wakes in a government office
finding in its fissures
an ovoid etched with seedling feathers.

The Spirit Maker

for Fiona McAllister (née McGill)

The night of her birth
diviners saw geese pull away to the heavens
before the fields moved towards gold.
Crouched beside fires
they traced portents in ash
lyrics of leaving in a scrawl of stars.

Brought up on a low lying river
her people taught her all they knew
roots for working
herbs for healing
the names of winds
the names she stitched to stars
at dusk the tie-up line, at dawn the tiller.

But none showed how to walk
the road she walks
dragging up from incalculable clay
sixteen hands of unbroken horse.
And no constellations of bone
revealed the air
she sculpted into breath
playing an Indian drum
softly the morning
her dark goose rose above a coral sun.

Leaving her in the weeping grounds
her only guide
a corm of light
found in the depths of a white seashell:
the migrant's call
a canticle of snow and garnets
crossing a wild magnetic northern shore.

The Day of the Angel

in memory Mary McGill (née Moran)

A week of waiting and yellow roses, of winter benediction
in artefacts of light – lustral shapes or communion of dust and water?
Cold consecration sealed in an origami of doubt.
The healer left you nothing but her tears and a royal covenant
of wings, *malaaikah, mal'ach,* messenger
or your own heart's breath diaphanous in lazuline and white?

It is four in the morning and you are still here; beyond
the night-struck glass a chaos of silence crowds eucalypt and beech.
Once a child's time-thronged cathedral, you always near
lambent lark-light hands signalling encouragement and reprimand
to family and those where bloodlines run less clear.
Now they lie calm and lovely in a galaxy of spheres.

I wish you had worn the earrings I wear today for this poem
symbol of an adopted land, the studied stars you bought
when I was twenty one; long before these hours of astral ambassadors,
of lucent pale-blue orbs, of a young saint's favourite flowers.
Before I saw feathers of morning and gold gleaming there
in the unflinching black of your daughter's black hair.

First Colour

in memory of Josephine McCotter (née McGill)

> *The earliest appear to be those with the short wavelengths,*
> *and therefore the colour blue*
>
> JULIA KRISTEVA, *Desire in Language*

You were the keeper of the shrine, serpentine prayers
and threadbare scapulars, small petitions
hidden in oak and myrtle under a mazarine moon.
In its forgiving light you knelt beside feral fires
a poetry of silhouettes unfolding on your hand a wind-wept rose.
Message from my namesake carried to a locked door.

Gift of sign stained with hope and nothing else
for what did you know of the smoky chamber
where a girl burnt an old photograph with alchemilla and marigold.
Reading your falling petals from afar
she saw the benevolence of ambient anomalies
glitter like a carcass of stars.

When stars and time faded
your seahorses (hippocami) surrendered to blunt reflexes
and bleached memories.
Our reflections waiting for ablution that could not come
sorrowed the intricacies of water
hanging like rhizomes from extended fingers.

If I could have closed them as later I closed your eyes
with more relief than decency demanded.
Wondering at the ease of it all
until your absence grew under a domed sky
stencilled with gold and carnadine. In that arithmetic of sound
the oud player heard the music of the spheres.

Mystical mathematics on the reddening ridge of day
conducting *acequias* to the Gate of the Pomegranate
theorems fractals surds in the place of cisterns.
A rebus for the faithful unravelled on fulgent scales of silver fishes.
Flashing through deep night above an old oratory
and the *rawda* where the nomad plants no orange trees.

Moving among the sparrows and Arabic script
you are there the morning the lions return to the courtyard.
From the orphanage of their ancient eyes
they watch you mix the secret of azure with saffron and rain.
It is here we will meet: standing in the space between.
A dark green silence has always been.

CLARE McCOTTER's haiku, tanka and haibun have been published in many parts of the world. She won The British Haiku Award 2017, The British Tanka Award 2013 and The HIS Dóchas Ireland Haiku Award 2011 and 2010. Her work has been included in the prestigious Norton anthology – *Haiku in English: The First Hundred Years*. Her longer poems have appeared in over thirty journals including *Abridged*, *Crannóg*, *Cyphers*, *Envoi*, *The Honest Ulsterman*, *Iota*, *The Interpreter's House* and *The Stinging Fly*. Awarded a Ph.D from the University of Ulster, she has also published numerous peer-reviewed articles on Belfast-born Beatrice Grimshaw's travel writing and fiction. Clare was one of three writers featured in *Measuring New Writers 1* (Dedalus Press). *Black Horse Running*, her first collection of haiku, tanka and haibun, was published in 2012 (Alba Publishing). *Revenant* is her first collection of longer poems. She has worked as a lecturer, a teacher of English, a psychiatric nurse and a full-time carer. Home is Kilrea, County Derry.

The Salmon Bookshop
& Literary Centre

Ennistymon, County Clare, Ireland